Top Ten AI Websites

Unlocking the Potential of Artificial Intelligence

By *Mike Bhangu*

Published by BB Productions
British Columbia, Canada
thinkingmanmike@gmail.com

Top Ten AI Websites

Unlocking the Potential of Artificial Intelligence

Table of Contents

Introduction

The field of Artificial Intelligence (AI) is rapidly evolving, shaping the future of various industries and impacting our daily lives in profound ways. As we navigate this dynamic landscape, it's crucial to have access to reliable and informative resources that can equip us with the knowledge and skills needed to thrive in the AI-powered future.

This diverse selection of websites equips you with the knowledge, tools, and connections needed to navigate the exciting world of AI. So, embark on your AI journey and unlock the potential of this transformative technology with our curated list!

You should read about this list of top ten AI websites for several reasons:

1. Stay informed and ahead of the curve: AI is rapidly evolving and having a significant impact on various industries and aspects of our lives. Reading about these websites will keep you informed about the latest trends, research, and developments in AI, allowing you to anticipate future changes and adapt accordingly.

2. Enhance your knowledge and skills: The websites listed offer a wealth of resources, including articles, tutorials, courses, and datasets, catering to diverse skill levels. Whether you're a beginner exploring the basics of AI or a seasoned professional seeking advanced techniques, these resources can help you deepen your understanding and acquire valuable skills.

3. Discover valuable tools and platforms: Many of the listed websites offer AI-powered tools and platforms that can be applied to various tasks, from scheduling meetings and analyzing medical symptoms to conducting legal research and building machine learning models. Reading about these tools can help you identify solutions to your specific needs and leverage AI to enhance your productivity and achieve your goals.

4. Connect with the AI community: Several websites listed foster vibrant communities of AI enthusiasts and experts. Engaging in these communities can help you connect with like-minded individuals, share your experiences, learn from each other, and collaborate on projects.

5. Make informed decisions about AI: Understanding the potential benefits and limitations of AI is crucial for making informed decisions about its use in your personal or professional life. Reading about these websites can help you assess the risks and opportunities associated with AI and make informed choices regarding its adoption.

6. Prepare for the future of work: AI is transforming the workforce, and understanding its implications is essential for career success. By exploring these AI websites, you can gain valuable insights into the skills and knowledge needed to thrive in the AI-powered future and prepare yourself for the changing landscape of work.

7. Expand your horizons and embrace innovation: AI is opening up new possibilities and revolutionizing various sectors. Exploring these websites

can spark your creativity, inspire you to think outside the box, and embrace the potential of AI for positive change and innovation.

In short, reading about these top ten AI websites can empower you to:

- Deepen your understanding of AI and its applications.

- Acquire valuable skills and knowledge for the AI-powered future.

- Access useful tools and platforms to enhance your productivity.

- Connect with the AI community and learn from others.

- Make informed decisions about AI use.

- Prepare for the future of work.

- Expand your horizons and embrace innovation.

So, embark on your journey into the world of AI today and unlock its potential for personal and professional success!

In no particular order, here are the top 10 most useful AI websites.

RunwayML: This website offers a diverse range of user-friendly AI tools for creative tasks like image generation, editing, and animation. It also features tools for audio manipulation, music composition, and code-based customization, making it ideal for artists, designers, and anyone interested in exploring the creative potential of AI.

OpenML: This platform promotes open-source development and collaboration in the field of machine learning. It provides access to a large repository of machine learning models, tools for tracking their performance, and a community forum for discussions and support. This makes it a valuable resource for researchers, developers, and anyone interested in learning about and applying machine learning techniques.

FastAI: This website offers high-quality online courses and resources covering various aspects of deep learning. It provides a hands-on approach to learning through practical exercises and projects, making it a great resource for anyone who wants to learn the fundamentals of deep learning and build practical AI applications.

X.ai: This website simplifies meeting scheduling by leveraging AI to find mutually agreeable times for participants. It integrates with calendar systems, handles rescheduling and cancellation requests, and offers features for team scheduling and managing meeting agendas. This makes it a time-saving tool for individuals and teams who want to streamline their meeting schedules.

Infermedica: This website uses AI to help users understand their symptoms and potential causes of medical conditions. It provides a symptom checker, suggests next steps, and offers educational resources about healthcare. While not a substitute for professional medical advice, it can be a valuable tool for self-diagnosis and empowering users to make informed decisions about their health.

Lexalytics: This website offers AI-powered solutions for legal research and analysis. It analyzes legal documents and identifies key legal issues, provides summaries and insights into complex legal matters, and predicts possible legal outcomes. This makes it a valuable tool for lawyers and legal professionals to streamline research, save time, and make informed decisions.

Dataiku: This platform is a collaborative data science and machine learning platform that empowers both data experts and domain experts to work together and integrate AI into their daily operations.

DataRobot: This AI platform takes the grunt work out of building and deploying impactful machine learning models. Think of it as a magic wand for data, automating the process from preparation to prediction. It empowers businesses of all sizes to unlock valuable insights from their data, solve real-world problems, and optimize operations without needing a team of data scientists.

Sentifi: This website analyzes social media conversations and news articles about financial markets. It identifies trends impacting stock prices, provides real-time insights and alerts, and integrates with other financial analysis tools. This makes it a valuable tool for investors who want to make informed decisions based on real-time data and insights.

Clara Labs: This website uses AI to analyze medical images and provide diagnostic support to radiologists. It identifies potential abnormalities and medical conditions with high accuracy, improving efficiency and accuracy in medical imaging analysis. This makes it a valuable tool for healthcare professionals to improve patient care and early detection of diseases.

As the field of AI continues to evolve, we can expect even more innovative and powerful tools to emerge in the future. By exploring the various options and understanding their capabilities, we can leverage the potential of AI to enhance our lives and make a positive impact on the world.

Criteria Used to Determine Top Ten

The following criteria were used to determine the top ten most useful AI websites:

Impact and reach: The website should have a significant impact on the field of AI and reach a large audience. This can be measured by factors such as the number of users, the number of models or tools available, the amount of media coverage, and the influence on other researchers and developers.

Versatility and range of applications: The website should offer a diverse range of AI tools and functionalities, catering to various user needs and applications. This can include text generation, translation, image recognition, music composition, audio manipulation, code-based customization, and other creative and practical tasks.

User-friendliness and accessibility: The website should be easy to use and accessible to users with varying levels of technical expertise. This can include a user-friendly interface, clear documentation, tutorials, and resources to help users get started and learn new skills.

Community and collaboration: The website should foster a strong and active community of users and developers. This can include forums, discussions, collaboration tools, and opportunities to share knowledge and resources.

Open-source and transparency: The website should promote open-source development and transparency. This can include making models and code publicly available, providing detailed documentation, and engaging with the community to address concerns and feedback.

Ethical considerations and responsible use: The website should promote the ethical use of AI and address potential biases, fairness, and privacy concerns. This can include clear guidelines, user controls, and transparency about the algorithms and data used.

Innovation and potential for future development: The website should be at the forefront of innovation and demonstrate potential for further development. This can include cutting-edge research, novel applications of AI, and plans for future features and functionalities.

By considering these criteria, we can identify the most valuable and impactful AI websites that contribute significantly to the field and empower users to explore and leverage the potential of AI technology.

It is important to note that this list is not exhaustive and may vary depending on individual needs and priorities. Additionally, the field of AI is constantly evolving, and new and exciting websites are emerging all the time. It is therefore important to stay informed and explore the latest developments to discover AI tools that can best meet your specific needs and interests.

Chapter 1: RunwayML

RunwayML takes a different approach to AI, focusing on empowering creativity through a diverse range of user-friendly AI tools. Its intuitive interface and interactive features make exploring the artistic potential of AI accessible to everyone, regardless of technical expertise.

Dive into a world of creative possibilities

RunwayML offers a plethora of AI tools for various creative endeavors, including:

1. Image: Image generation, editing, and animation; style transfer; background removal; and more.

2. Audio: Music composition, sound design, voice manipulation, and audio editing.

3. Video: Video editing, animation, and effects.

4. Code: Custom scripting for advanced manipulation and experimentation.

These tools are designed to be intuitive and playful, allowing users to explore their creative visions with ease. RunwayML provides various templates and pre-built projects to get started, while also offering ample opportunities for experimentation and customization.

User-friendly features and resources

RunwayML focuses on making AI-powered creativity accessible and enjoyable for everyone. Several features contribute to this:

1. Drag-and-drop interface: A simple and intuitive interface makes the tools accessible to users with varying technical backgrounds.

2. Real-time interaction: Users can see the results of their changes instantly, fostering a dynamic and interactive creative process.

3. Tutorials and documentation: Comprehensive tutorials and documentation provide clear instructions and guidance for using the various tools.

4. Community: A vibrant community of artists and designers shares inspiration, tips, and feedback.

These features allow users to learn quickly, overcome technical barriers, and focus on unleashing their creative potential.

Collaboration and co-creation

RunwayML fosters a collaborative environment where artists and designers can work together to create stunning visual and audio experiences. The platform's features enable:

1. Real-time co-creation: Multiple users can work on a project simultaneously, seeing each other's changes and collaborating in real-time.

2. Sharing and remixing: Users can share their creations with others, allowing for remixing, building upon existing work, and fostering new creative directions.

3. Community projects: RunwayML hosts regular community projects where artists and designers collaborate on specific themes and challenges.

4. This emphasis on collaboration encourages creative exchange, sparks new ideas, and pushes the boundaries of what is possible with AI-powered creativity.

Empowering new forms of storytelling and expression

RunwayML's tools are not just for individual artists; they also have the potential to revolutionize storytelling and expression across various fields. Here are some examples:

1. Film and animation: Creating stunning visuals and animations for films, TV shows, and video games.

2. Marketing and advertising: Developing engaging and interactive marketing campaigns.

3. Education: Creating interactive learning experiences and engaging students in new ways.

4. Healthcare: Providing tools for medical visualization and patient education.

By democratizing access to AI-powered creative tools, RunwayML empowers individuals and organizations to explore new ways of communicating, engaging, and expressing themselves.

A bright future for creative AI

RunwayML is at the forefront of the movement to democratize AI for creative purposes. Its platform has already empowered countless artists and designers to create innovative and inspiring work. As AI technology continues to evolve, RunwayML is positioned to play an even more significant role in shaping the future of creative expression.

Looking ahead, RunwayML is focusing on:

- Expanding its library of AI tools: Adding new and innovative tools to cater to a wider range of creative needs.

- Enhancing user experience: Making the platform even more intuitive and accessible to users with varying technical backgrounds.

- Fostering collaboration: Providing tools and resources to encourage artists and designers to work together and create collaboratively.

- Exploring responsible AI development: Ensuring that AI is used ethically and responsibly in the creative realm.

With its commitment to pushing the boundaries of AI-powered creativity, RunwayML holds immense promise for revolutionizing how we create, consume, and interact with art and media in the future.

WEBSITE: https://runwayml.com

Chapter 2: OpenML

OpenML is a unique platform that promotes open-source development and collaboration in the field of machine learning. It provides a central hub for researchers, developers, and data scientists to share and collaborate on machine learning models, datasets, and tools. This collaborative approach fosters innovation, accelerates research progress, and makes machine learning more accessible to everyone.

A repository of machine learning knowledge

OpenML serves as a vast repository of valuable machine learning resources, including:

1. Machine learning models: A diverse collection of pre-trained models for various tasks, readily available for download and experimentation.

2. Datasets: A curated collection of datasets covering various domains, enabling researchers to train and evaluate their own models.

3. Evaluation tools: Standardized tools for evaluating the performance of machine learning models, facilitating fair comparison and analysis.

4. Workflow templates: Pre-built workflow templates for common machine learning tasks, helping users get started quickly.

This centralized repository allows researchers and developers to leverage existing resources, build upon each other's work, and avoid reinventing the wheel.

Collaboration and knowledge sharing

OpenML goes beyond a simple repository by fostering a vibrant community of collaborators. Key features include:

1. Model sharing: Users can upload their own trained models and share them with the community, promoting knowledge sharing and reuse.

2. Collaborative workflows: Users can collaborate on building and refining machine learning models, accelerating research progress.

3. Discussions and forums: OpenML provides forums for discussions and Q&A, allowing users to seek help, share experiences, and learn from each other.

4. Events and workshops: OpenML hosts regular events and workshops to promote knowledge sharing and collaboration within the community.

This collaborative environment facilitates learning, problem-solving, and innovation, pushing the boundaries of what is possible in machine learning.

Openness and transparency

OpenML is built around the principles of open-source development and transparency. This is evident in:

1. Open-source platform: The platform's code is publicly available, allowing anyone to contribute and improve its functionalities.

2. Open data and models: Many datasets and models on OpenML are available under open-source licenses, promoting reproducibility and scientific progress.

3. Collaborative governance: OpenML is governed by a community-based steering committee, ensuring that the platform remains open and accessible to all.

This focus on openness and transparency fosters trust within the community and encourages responsible development and use of machine learning technology.

Impact and future potential

OpenML has had a significant impact on the field of machine learning by:

1. Accelerating research progress: By providing a central hub for sharing resources and collaborating, OpenML has facilitated

faster development and advancement of machine learning techniques.

2. Democratizing machine learning: By making resources and tools readily available, OpenML has lowered the barrier to entry for machine learning and empowered individuals and organizations to leverage its potential.

3. Promoting ethical development: OpenML's commitment to open-source principles encourages transparency and accountability in the development and deployment of machine learning models.

Looking ahead

OpenML is poised to play an even more crucial role in the future of machine learning. The platform is actively expanding its capabilities by:

- Adding new features: This includes support for new model formats, data types, and evaluation metrics.

- Enhancing collaboration tools: This will facilitate more seamless and efficient collaboration among researchers and developers.

- Exploring emerging areas: OpenML is exploring integration with new technologies like AI explainability and responsible AI development.

By continuing to foster openness, collaboration, and innovation, OpenML is paving the way for a more accessible, inclusive, and ethical future of machine learning.

WEBSITE: https://www.openml.org

Chapter 3: FastAI

FastAI offers a unique approach to learning deep learning, focusing on practical hands-on experience rather than theoretical knowledge. Its high-quality online courses and resources provide students with the necessary tools and skills to build real-world deep learning applications, making it a valuable resource for aspiring practitioners.

Hands-on learning with real-world projects

FastAI's cornerstone lies in its practical approach to learning deep learning. Instead of relying solely on lectures and theoretical concepts, the platform emphasizes:

1. Project-based learning: Students learn by working on real-world projects from various domains, such as image classification, natural language processing, and computer vision.
2. Coding exercises: Each project involves hands-on coding exercises, allowing students to apply the learned concepts and build their own deep learning models.
3. Rapid prototyping: FastAI encourages rapid prototyping, allowing students to experiment with different approaches and quickly iterate on their projects.

This hands-on approach provides a deeper understanding of deep learning principles and empowers students to confidently apply their skills in real-world scenarios.

Accessible and engaging learning experience

FastAI strives to make deep learning accessible to everyone, regardless of their prior technical background. Key features include:

1. Clear and concise explanations: The course materials are presented in a clear and concise manner, making complex concepts easier to grasp.
2. Interactive learning environment: FastAI utilizes interactive Jupyter notebooks, allowing students to experiment with code and see the results immediately.
3. Community support: A vibrant online community provides support, answers questions, and helps students overcome challenges.
4. Flexible learning options: FastAI offers various learning options, including free online courses, paid workshops, and self-paced learning resources.

These features cater to different learning styles and provide students with the flexibility and support they need to succeed in their deep learning journey.

Focus on practical applications

FastAI emphasizes the practical applications of deep learning, equipping students with the skills to solve real-world problems. This is evident in:

1. Project selection: Courses and projects focus on real-world applications across various domains, such as healthcare, finance, and environmental science.

2. Industry-relevant skills: FastAI teaches relevant skills in demand within the industry, such as data preparation, model training, and evaluation.

3. Collaboration with industry partners: FastAI collaborates with various industries to ensure its courses remain relevant and cater to current industry needs.

This focus on practical applications ensures that students graduate with the necessary skills to be successful in the workforce and contribute to meaningful advancements in their chosen fields.

Shaping the future of deep learning education

FastAI is at the forefront of transforming deep learning education. By prioritizing hands-on learning, practical applications, and accessibility, the platform empowers individuals to leverage the power of deep learning and contribute to its advancement.

Looking ahead, FastAI is committed to:

- Expanding its course offerings: This includes developing new courses covering emerging deep learning techniques and applications.

- Enhancing the learning experience: This involves utilizing cutting-edge tools and technologies to create even more engaging and interactive learning experiences.

- Promoting diversity and inclusion: FastAI actively works to make its learning resources accessible to individuals from all backgrounds.

- Contributing to responsible AI development: FastAI integrates ethical considerations into its courses, encouraging students to develop and deploy deep learning models responsibly.

By continuing to innovate and lead the way in deep learning education, FastAI is shaping the future of the field and empowering a new generation of deep learning practitioners to tackle the challenges and opportunities of tomorrow.

WEBSITE: https://www.fast.ai

Chapter 4: X.ai

X.ai demonstrates the power of AI by simplifying and streamlining the often-tedious process of meeting scheduling. Its AI-powered system automatically finds mutually agreeable times for participants, eliminating the need for endless email exchanges and back-and-forth communication.

Find the perfect time, every time

X.ai solves the common problem of finding a meeting time that works for everyone involved. Its key features include:

- Calendar integration: Connects seamlessly with existing calendars, automatically pulling availability information.

- AI-powered scheduling: Uses AI algorithms to suggest mutually agreeable times based on participants' schedules and preferences.

- Automatic negotiation: Handles rescheduling and cancellation requests efficiently, minimizing back-and-forth communication.

- Time zone management: Accounts for different time zones, ensuring everyone can participate regardless of their location.

This combination of features eliminates the need for manual scheduling, saving individuals and teams valuable time and effort.

Beyond scheduling: Features for enhanced meeting productivity

X.ai goes beyond simply finding meeting times. It offers additional features to enhance meeting productivity, including:

1. Meeting agenda creation: Automatically generates a meeting agenda based on the meeting's purpose and participants.

2. Meeting notes: Provides a platform to take notes, share action items, and track progress.

3. Follow-up reminders: Sends reminders to participants before and after the meeting.

4. Integrations: Integrates with other productivity tools, such as Zoom and Slack, for a seamless workflow.

These features ensure that meetings are well-organized, productive, and actionable, maximizing the value of everyone's time.

User-friendliness and accessibility

X.ai prioritizes user-friendliness and accessibility for everyone, regardless of their technical expertise. This is evident in:

1. Intuitive interface: Easy-to-use interface with clear instructions and guidance.
2. Multiple access options: Available as a web app, mobile app, and desktop application.

3. Customization options: Allows users to personalize their settings and preferences.

4. Multilingual support: Available in various languages to cater to a global audience.

These factors make X.ai a user-friendly tool that can be readily adopted by individuals and organizations of all sizes.

Impact and future potential

X.ai has had a significant impact on how we schedule meetings. Its AI-powered solution has:

1. Increased productivity: Saved individuals and teams countless hours by automating the scheduling process.

2. Reduced stress: Eliminated the frustration and wasted time associated with manual scheduling.

3. Improved communication: Encouraged clear and concise communication regarding meeting availability and preferences.

4. Enhanced meeting attendance: Increased meeting attendance by ensuring everyone can find a convenient time.

Looking ahead

X.ai is poised to play an even greater role in shaping the future of meeting culture. The platform is actively exploring:

- Advanced AI algorithms: Developing even more sophisticated AI algorithms to improve scheduling accuracy and efficiency.

- Integration with additional tools: Integrating with a wider range of productivity and collaboration tools.

- Meeting optimization: Exploring features to further enhance meeting effectiveness and engagement.

- Focus on responsible AI development: Ensuring AI technology is used ethically and responsibly within the meeting scheduling context.

By continuing to innovate and push the boundaries of AI-powered scheduling, X.ai is paving the way for a more productive, efficient, and collaborative working environment for everyone.

WEBSITE: X.ai

Chapter 5: Infermedica

Infermedica empowers individuals by providing AI-assisted medical diagnosis support. Its platform utilizes sophisticated algorithms to analyze symptoms and suggest potential causes, helping individuals understand their health concerns and make informed decisions about seeking medical attention.

AI-driven symptom analysis

Infermedica's core functionality lies in its AI-powered symptom analysis engine. This engine analyzes user-reported symptoms and medical history, utilizing a vast database of medical knowledge and clinical guidelines to:

1. Identify potential medical conditions: Based on the reported symptoms, the platform suggests a list of possible medical conditions that could be causing the symptoms.

2. Provide information about each condition: For each suggested condition, Infermedica offers concise and informative descriptions, explaining the symptoms, causes, diagnostic tests, and treatment options.

3. Estimate the likelihood of each condition: Based on the user's specific symptom combination and medical history, the platform assigns a probability score to each suggested condition, helping users prioritize their concerns.

This AI-driven analysis empowers individuals to understand their symptoms better and make informed decisions about their next steps.

Empowering self-diagnosis and education

While Infermedica is not intended to replace professional medical diagnosis, it offers valuable tools for self-diagnosis and education. These include:

1. Symptom checker: Users can input their symptoms and receive a personalized list of potential causes and information about each condition.

2. Medical encyclopedia: The platform provides access to a comprehensive medical encyclopedia with detailed information about various medical conditions, symptoms, treatments, and medications.

3. Educational resources: Infermedica offers various educational resources, such as articles, videos, and infographics, to help users understand health topics and make informed decisions.

These tools help individuals navigate the often-complex world of healthcare and empowers them to take an active role in their health management.

Promoting responsible use

Infermedica emphasizes responsible use and encourages collaboration with healthcare professionals. Key features include:

1. Disclaimer: The platform clearly states that it should not be used for self-diagnosis or treatment decisions and encourages users to seek professional medical advice.

2. Integration with healthcare providers: Infermedica offers tools for healthcare providers to integrate the platform into their workflow, allowing them to utilize the AI-powered analysis to enhance their diagnostic process and patient care.

3. Compliance with medical regulations: The platform adheres to strict medical regulations and ethical guidelines to ensure data privacy and responsible use of AI technology.

This commitment to responsible use and collaboration fosters trust and ensures that Infermedica serves as a valuable tool for individuals and healthcare professionals alike.

Impact and future potential

Infermedica has had a significant impact on the healthcare landscape by:

1. Democratizing access to medical information: Empowering individuals with AI-powered symptom analysis and comprehensive medical knowledge.

2. Promoting early diagnosis: Assisting individuals in identifying potential health concerns and seeking medical attention early.

3. Empowering informed decision-making: Helping individuals understand their health concerns and make informed choices about their healthcare.

4. Enhancing healthcare efficiency: Supporting healthcare providers with AI-powered tools for improved diagnosis and patient care.

Looking ahead, Infermedica is committed to:

- Expanding its medical knowledge base: Continuously updating its database with new medical information and research findings.

- Enhancing its AI algorithms: Improving the accuracy and reliability of the symptom analysis engine.

- Developing new features: Exploring features like medication interactions and personalized health recommendations.

- Expanding international reach: Making the platform accessible to individuals and healthcare providers worldwide.

By continuing to innovate and push the boundaries of AI-assisted medical diagnosis, Infermedica has the potential to revolutionize healthcare delivery and empower individuals to take control of their health and well-being.

WEBSITE: https://infermedica.com

Chapter 6: Lexalytics

Lexalytics is transforming the legal landscape by offering AI-powered solutions for legal research and analysis. Its platform facilitates efficient and insightful legal research, empowering lawyers and legal professionals to navigate the complexities of legal documents and make informed decisions.

Unlocking the power of legal language

Lexalytics utilizes advanced AI techniques to analyze and extract valuable insights from massive volumes of legal text. Its key functionalities include:

1. Automated legal research: The platform searches and analyzes legal documents, case law, and other legal resources based on specific user queries and keywords.

2. Identification of key legal issues: Lexalytics identifies and highlights the most relevant legal issues and arguments within the analyzed documents.

3. Predictive analysis: The platform utilizes AI algorithms to predict the potential outcomes of legal matters based on similar cases and historical data.

4. Sentiment analysis: Lexalytics analyzes the sentiment of legal documents, providing insights into the author's perspective and potential biases.

These capabilities enable legal professionals to conduct research more efficiently, gain deeper understanding of complex legal issues, and make informed decisions with greater confidence.

Beyond keyword searches: Deeper insights and context

Lexalytics goes beyond simply searching for keywords. Its AI-powered analysis offers:

1. Contextual understanding: The platform analyzes not just keywords, but also the context in which they appear, providing a more nuanced understanding of the legal issues at hand.

2. Relationship identification: Lexalytics identifies relationships between different legal concepts and entities, allowing for a more holistic view of the legal landscape.

3. Trend analysis: The platform analyzes trends across legal documents and case law, providing insights into evolving legal interpretations and potential legal risks.

This depth of analysis empowers legal professionals to identify patterns, anticipate future legal developments, and make strategic decisions with a better understanding of the legal landscape.

Streamlining legal workflows and enhancing productivity

Lexalytics offers features that enhance the workflow and productivity of legal professionals:

1. Automated document summarization: The platform automatically generates summaries of legal documents, saving time and effort for lawyers and researchers.

2. Case comparison: Lexalytics facilitates easy comparison of similar cases, allowing users to quickly identify relevant precedents and legal arguments.

3. Collaboration tools: The platform offers features for collaboration and knowledge sharing among team members, enhancing communication and efficiency.

4. Integration with legal research platforms: Lexalytics integrates with popular legal research platforms, providing seamless access to its AI-powered analysis within existing workflows.

These features help legal professionals save time, improve workflow efficiency, and make better use of their valuable time and expertise.

Impact and future potential

Lexalytics has revolutionized legal research by:

1. Improving legal research efficiency: Enabling legal professionals to find relevant information quickly and accurately.

2. Enhancing legal analysis: Providing deeper insights into complex legal issues and potential outcomes.

3. Reducing risk and improving decision-making: Empowering legal professionals to make informed decisions with a greater understanding of the legal landscape.

4. Democratizing access to legal knowledge: Making legal research tools more accessible to a broader range of individuals and organizations.

Looking ahead, Lexalytics is focused on:

- Expanding its legal knowledge base: Continuously adding new legal data and resources to its platform.

- Developing advanced AI algorithms: Improving the accuracy and efficiency of its legal analysis capabilities.

- Exploring new applications: Investigating the use of AI for legal tasks such as contract review, e-discovery, and legal writing assistance.

- Promoting ethical and responsible use of AI: Ensuring that AI technology is used ethically and responsibly in the legal field.

By continuing to innovate and push the boundaries of AI-powered legal research, Lexalytics promises to further revolutionize the legal industry and empower legal professionals to achieve greater success and efficiency.

WEBSITE: https://www.lexalytics.com

Chapter 7: Dataiku

Dataiku empowers organizations of all sizes to leverage the power of data science by offering a unified platform that simplifies and streamlines the entire data science lifecycle. From data preparation and modeling to deployment and monitoring, Dataiku provides a comprehensive solution that makes data science accessible to a wider range of users.

A single platform for the entire data science lifecycle

Dataiku's core offering lies in its unified platform, encompassing the entire data science workflow:

1. Data preparation: Dataiku provides tools for data cleaning, wrangling, and transformation, ensuring high-quality data ready for analysis.

2. Model development: The platform offers a variety of machine learning algorithms and tools for building, training, and evaluating models.

3. Model deployment: Dataiku facilitates the deployment of trained models into production environments, enabling real-world applications.

4. Model monitoring: The platform provides tools for monitoring model performance and detecting potential issues, ensuring reliable and accurate predictions.

This centralized approach eliminates the need for switching between disparate tools and streamlines the data science process, saving time and resources.

Collaboration and knowledge sharing

Dataiku fosters a collaborative environment for data scientists and other stakeholders. Key features include:

- Collaborative workspace: Teams can work together on projects in a shared environment, facilitating knowledge sharing and communication.

- Version control: Dataiku provides version control for data, code, and models, ensuring reproducibility and traceability.

- Interactive dashboards: The platform offers interactive dashboards for visualizing data and model results, enabling clear communication and insights.

- Centralized repository: Dataiku serves as a central repository for data, models, and documentation, promoting best practices and
- knowledge sharing.

These features enable effective collaboration across teams, breaking down silos and accelerating the data science process.

Scalability and flexibility

Dataiku scales to meet the needs of organizations of all sizes. Its key features include:

1. Cloud-based platform: The platform is available as a cloud-based service, eliminating the need for infrastructure management.

2. Open-source integration: Dataiku integrates seamlessly with various open-source tools and libraries, providing flexibility and customization.

3. API access: The platform offers API access, allowing developers to build custom applications and integrations.

4. Role-based access control: Dataiku provides role-based access control to ensure data security and governance.

This scalability and flexibility make Dataiku suitable for various use cases and organizations, from small startups to large enterprises.

Impact and future potential

Dataiku has had a significant impact on the data science landscape by:

1. Democratizing data science: Making data science more accessible to a broader range of users by offering a user-friendly platform and simplifying the data science workflow.

2. Accelerating innovation: Enabling organizations to develop and deploy data-driven solutions faster and more efficiently.

3. Enhancing collaboration: Fostering a collaborative environment for data scientists and other stakeholders, leading to improved communication and knowledge sharing.

4. Promoting responsible AI development: Encouraging ethical and responsible use of AI by providing tools for model monitoring and bias detection.

Looking ahead, Dataiku is focused on:

- Expanding its platform capabilities: Adding new features and functionalities to support emerging data science trends and technologies.

- Enhancing AI explainability: Providing tools and features to explain how models make decisions, increasing transparency and trust.

- Promoting data literacy: Offering educational resources and training programs to improve data literacy across organizations.

- Collaborating with research institutions: Partnering with research institutions to advance the field of data science and develop new AI solutions.

By continuing to innovate and lead the way in democratizing data science, Dataiku has the potential to unlock the power of data for organizations of all sizes and drive advancements in various fields.

WEBSITE: https://www.dataiku.com

Chapter 8: DataRobot

DataRobot empowers individuals and organizations of all sizes to leverage the power of machine learning through its automated machine learning platform. This platform automates various aspects of the machine learning process, making it accessible to users with varying levels of technical expertise.

Automating the machine learning lifecycle

DataRobot automates various stages of the machine learning lifecycle, including:

1. Data preparation: The platform automatically cleans, wrangles, and transforms data, minimizing manual effort and ensuring data quality.

2. Feature engineering: DataRobot automatically generates relevant features from raw data, eliminating the need for manual feature engineering expertise.

3. Model selection: The platform automatically builds and evaluates a wide range of machine learning models, choosing the best performing model for the specific task.

4. Model deployment: DataRobot automates model deployment into production environments, enabling real-time predictions and decision-making.

5. Model monitoring: The platform continuously monitors deployed models, detecting potential issues and ensuring reliable and accurate predictions.

This automation frees up valuable time and resources for users, allowing them to focus on interpreting results and driving business value from their machine learning models.

User-friendly interface and low barrier to entry
DataRobot prioritizes user-friendliness and accessibility. Its key features include:

1. Drag-and-drop interface: The platform utilizes a visual and intuitive drag-and-drop interface, making it easy for users with no coding experience to build and deploy machine learning models.

2. Pre-built templates: DataRobot offers pre-built templates for common machine learning tasks, further simplifying the process for users.

3. Extensive documentation and support: The platform provides comprehensive documentation, tutorials, and support resources to help users get started and overcome challenges.

4. Flexible deployment options: DataRobot offers various deployment options, including on-premise, cloud-based, and hybrid deployments, catering to diverse needs and preferences.

These features lower the barrier to entry for machine learning, making it accessible to a wider audience and enabling individuals and organizations to leverage its power without the need for extensive technical expertise.

Explainability and interpretability

DataRobot emphasizes the importance of model explainability and interpretability. Key features include:

1. Model insights: The platform provides detailed insights into how models make decisions, allowing users to understand the rationale behind the predictions.

2. Feature importance: DataRobot identifies the most important features that contribute to the model's predictions, helping users understand what drives the results.

3. Counterfactual analysis: The platform provides counterfactual analysis, which allows users to explore how different data points would have affected the model's predictions.

These features enhance user trust in the models and enable them to interpret and explain the results to stakeholders, fostering transparency and accountability.

Impact and future potential

DataRobot has significantly impacted the machine learning landscape by:

1. Democratizing machine learning: Making machine learning accessible to a broader range of users, regardless of their technical expertise.

2. Accelerating innovation: Enabling organizations to develop and deploy machine learning solutions faster and more efficiently.

3. Enhancing transparency and trust: Providing features for model explainability and interpretability, building trust in machine learning models.

4. Promoting responsible AI development: Offering tools for bias detection and fairness analysis, encouraging responsible use of AI technology.

Looking ahead, DataRobot is focused on:

• Expanding its automation capabilities: Automating even more aspects of the machine learning process, further reducing manual effort.

• Improving model explainability: Developing new and innovative techniques for explaining how models make decisions.

- Expanding its platform ecosystem: Integrating with additional tools and platforms to provide a comprehensive solution for all machine learning needs.

- Promoting responsible AI governance: Advocating for ethical and responsible use of AI technology and developing frameworks for governance.

By continuing to innovate and democratize machine learning, DataRobot holds immense potential to empower individuals and organizations to unlock the power of data and drive advancements across various industries.

WEBSITE: https://www.datarobot.com

Chapter 9: Sentifi

The financial markets are a cacophony of information - news headlines, analyst reports, social media chatter. But for most investors, deciphering this symphony of data is a daunting task. This is where Sentifi steps in, acting as your personal translator, turning the market's whispers into actionable insights.

Traditional investment research often relies on lagging indicators and filtered data, leaving investors vulnerable to sudden market shifts. They grapple with:

1. Information Overload: A deluge of data from disparate sources makes it difficult to identify relevant signals amidst the noise.

2. Limited Scope: Traditional analysis often focuses on historical data and overlooks the real-time pulse of the market, missing out on emerging trends.

3. Subjectivity: Human analysts can be biased by their own experiences and preconceptions, leading to misinterpretations of market signals.

Sentifi cuts through the noise with its AI-powered platform, analyzing millions of social media conversations and news articles daily. It:

1. Harnesses the Power of the Crowd: Sentifi goes beyond traditional financial data, tapping into the collective intelligence of social media, where investors share opinions, insights, and even rumors that can impact market sentiment.

2. Identifies Trends in Real-time: Its AI algorithms process vast amounts of data in real-time, detecting emerging trends and shifts in sentiment before they hit the mainstream.

3. Provides Actionable Insights: Sentifi doesn't just tell you what's happening; it translates the data into actionable insights, like identifying stocks with rising positive sentiment or predicting potential market corrections.

Sentifi's Value Proposition

Sentifi is more than just a data analysis tool; it's a game-changer for investors by:

1. Democratizing Access to Market Insights: Sentifi empowers individual investors with the same level of data and insights as large institutional firms, leveling the playing field.

2. Enhancing Decision-making: Real-time insights allow investors to react quickly to market changes, make informed investment decisions, and capitalize on emerging opportunities.

3. Reducing Risk: By identifying potential market corrections and negative sentiment, Sentifi helps investors mitigate risk and protect their portfolios.

Seeing Sentifi in Action

- The Meme Stock Surge: Sentifi identified the growing buzz around meme stocks on social media weeks before they exploded, allowing investors to capitalize on the trend.

- The Unexpected Downturn: By analyzing the shift in sentiment on Twitter, Sentifi predicted a market correction before it hit the mainstream news, helping investors adjust their positions accordingly.

In the fast-paced world of finance, having a finger on the pulse of the market is crucial. Sentifi's AI-powered insights empower investors to navigate the market's whispers, make informed decisions, and ultimately, gain a competitive edge. So, tune out the noise and listen to what the market is truly saying – Sentifi is here to translate.

WEBSITE: https://sentifi-html.pages.dev

Chapter 10 Clara Labs

Imagine a world where medical images weren't just static snapshots, but dynamic portals revealing hidden patterns and abnormalities the naked eye might miss. This is the reality Clara Labs ushers in, leveraging the power of AI to empower radiologists and revolutionize healthcare.

The Challenge

Radiologists are the gatekeepers of medical imaging, their keen eyes interpreting scans to diagnose diseases and guide treatment. But the sheer volume of images, coupled with their intricate details, can be overwhelming. Fatigue, time constraints, and inherent human limitations can lead to missed diagnoses, impacting patient care.

The AI Ally

Clara Labs steps in as a tireless AI companion, augmenting radiologists' vision and decision-making. Its advanced algorithms analyze images, identifying and highlighting potential abnormalities with remarkable accuracy. This includes:

1. Tumor detection: Early detection of tumors, even subtle ones, can be life-saving. Clara Labs excels at spotting suspicious lesions in various organs, like lungs, breasts, and brains.

2. Fracture identification: Fractures can be difficult to discern, especially in complex bones. Clara Labs pinpoints fractures with

precision, ensuring timely treatment and preventing complications.

3. Hemorrhage detection: Internal bleeding can be a medical emergency. Clara Labs identifies subtle signs of hemorrhage in scans, allowing for prompt intervention.

Beyond Detection

Clara Labs goes beyond simply pointing out abnormalities. It provides valuable insights, such as:

1. Lesion characterization: Clara Labs analyzes the size, shape, and texture of lesions, providing radiologists with crucial information for differential diagnosis.

2. Treatment planning: By predicting the likelihood of malignancy or the aggressiveness of a tumor, Clara Labs helps guide treatment decisions and personalize patient care.

3. Workflow optimization: By prioritizing critical cases and automating repetitive tasks, Clara Labs frees up valuable time for radiologists to focus on complex diagnoses.

The Future of Medical Imaging

Clara Labs represents a paradigm shift in medical imaging. It's not about replacing radiologists, but rather empowering them with a powerful AI partner. This collaboration will lead to:

- Improved diagnostic accuracy: Early and accurate diagnoses translate to better patient outcomes and reduced healthcare costs.

- Enhanced efficiency: Streamlined workflows and faster turnaround times benefit both patients and healthcare providers.

- Personalized medicine: AI-driven insights pave the way for tailored treatment plans and improved patient care.

Clara Labs is not just a software; it's a beacon of hope in the healthcare landscape. By augmenting human expertise with the power of AI, it paves the way for a future where medical imaging becomes a transformative tool for early disease detection, improved patient care, and ultimately, healthier lives.

WEBSITE: https://claralabs.com

Conclusion: The Future of AI-powered Solutions

The tools and platforms discussed in this book represent only a glimpse into the vast landscape of AI-powered solutions rapidly transforming various aspects of our lives. From streamlining creative processes and legal research to democratizing access to medical diagnosis and data science, AI is demonstrably shaping the future across diverse fields.

As AI technology continues to evolve, we can expect even more profound and transformative applications:

1. Enhanced creativity and human-machine collaboration: AI will further empower artists, designers, and other creative professionals by automating tedious tasks, sparking new ideas, and facilitating seamless human-machine collaboration.

2. Personalized and adaptive learning experiences: AI-powered educational platforms will tailor learning experiences to individual needs and learning styles, maximizing engagement and promoting personalized learning paths.

3. Democratized access to healthcare: AI-powered tools will increase access to healthcare in underserved communities, providing remote diagnosis, personalized treatment plans, and improved healthcare outcomes.

4. Sustainable and resilient infrastructure: AI will optimize energy usage, manage resources efficiently, and predict potential disruptions, leading to more sustainable and resilient infrastructure.

5. Responsible and ethical AI development: As AI becomes increasingly integrated into our society, the need for responsible and ethical development will be paramount. This necessitates transparent algorithms, fair data practices, and robust security measures to mitigate potential biases and ensure ethical AI use.

While embracing the exciting possibilities of AI, it is crucial to acknowledge and address potential challenges:

1. Bias and fairness: AI models can perpetuate existing biases in data, leading to unfair and discriminatory outcomes. Addressing bias through diverse datasets, algorithmic fairness auditing, and human oversight is crucial.

2. Explainability and interpretability: Understanding how AI models make decisions is essential for building trust and accountability. Continued research and development in explainable AI techniques will be crucial.

3. Job displacement and economic inequality: While AI automates some tasks, it also creates new opportunities. Reskilling and

upskilling initiatives will be necessary to ensure a smooth transition for individuals impacted by automation.

4. Privacy and security concerns: AI applications raise concerns about data privacy and security. Robust data protection regulations and user control over personal data are essential.

Navigating the future of AI requires a collaborative approach involving researchers, developers, policymakers, and the public. By fostering open dialogue, addressing challenges proactively, and prioritizing responsible development, we can harness the power of AI for the benefit of all.

This book serves as a call to action, inviting readers to explore the potential of AI-powered solutions in their own fields and contribute to shaping a future where AI empowers creativity, promotes innovation, and drives progress towards a more equitable and sustainable world.